Praise for the novels of Haywood Smith

"Hilarious and wise."

—*Dorothea Benton Frank*

"A veritable gold mine of Southern homespun homilies where the Ya Ya Sisterhood would feel right at home."

—*Booklist*

"Strong characters and irrepressible wit; snapshots of Southern living will charm even the hardest-hearted Yankee."

—*Publishers Weekly*

Quotes from
Haywood Smith's

Ladies of the Lake

"The only people who ought to get married are the ones who absolutely, positively can't help it."

"Plan all you want, but God has a sense of humor."

"When it comes to love, give me a good dose of illusion every time."

The Twelve
Sacred Traditions
of Magnificent
Mothers-in-Law

Haywood Smith

Smyrna, Georgia

BelleBooks, Inc.
ISBN 978-0-9821756-0-6
The Twelve Sacred Traditions of Magnificent Mothers-in-Law

Published by: BelleBooks, Inc.   •   PO Box 67 • Smyrna, GA 30081
We at BelleBooks enjoy hearing from readers. You can contact us at the
address above or at BelleBooks@BelleBooks.com
Visit our website – www.BelleBooks.com

First Edition April 2009

10 9 8 7 6 5 4 3 2 1

Cover design: Debra Dixon
Interior design: Martha Crockett
Interior illustrations: Haywood Smith

Cover Photo: ©Victoria Shaad / Dreamstime.com

This book is dedicated to my gorgeous,

amazing daughter-in-law

Courtney

Haywood Smith

The Twelve Sacred Traditions of Magnificent Mothers-in-Law is a very Southern mother-in-law's humorous advice to mothers-in-law everywhere, including tried and tested tips on:

- How to Bite Your Tongue
- Minding Your Own Business
- Why You Shouldn't Tell his New Bride about that Time in Third Grade When He Threw Up on Stage while Playing a Sheep in the Christmas Pageant
- and much more!

Haywood Smith's Southern novel, *The Red Hat Club*, made the New York Times bestseller list. *The Red Hat Club Rides Again* debuted at #26 on the *New York Times* list. The paperback edition of *Queen Bee of Mimosa Branch* appeared on both the *USA Today*'s list and the *New York Times* extended bestseller list. *Wedding Belles*, Smith's most recent novel, was released in September 2008 from St. Martin's Press, New York. *Wedding Belles* was selected as one of the best audio books of 2008 by Publishers Weekly.

Visit Haywood at www.haywoodsmith.net

Haywood Smith

The Twelve Sacred Traditions of Magnificent Mothers-in-Law

ᏧᏣ ᏧᏣ ᏧᏣ ᏧᏣ ᏧᏣ

"Nobody gets any brownie points for loving people who are easy to love. Difficult people are God's sandpaper. They'll rub those rough edges off you and let you prove your faith."

—*My Granny Bess*

ᏧᏣ ᏧᏣ ᏧᏣ ᏧᏣ ᏧᏣ

"Mothers-in-Law Anonymous"

We, the official and unofficial members of Mothers-in-law Anonymous, in order to form a more perfect union with our married children and their spouses, to establish tolerance, insure domestic tranquility, disprove all those bad-mother-in-law jokes, promote the general welfare, and secure the blessings of our sons- and daughters-in-law, do ordain and establish these Twelve Sacred Traditions for Magnificent Mothers-in-law for ourselves and our posterity.

No animals were injured in the production of these traditions, but an entire tray of sandwiches from Henri's Bakery in Atlanta and a jumbo jug of sunny rosé were consumed, followed by a box of éclairs and some really nice Kona coffee.

Though half of us had bad mothers-in-law, and a few had some seriously sad mothers-in-law, we've done our best to keep our guidelines positive.

In the interest of flow and brevity, we've used the term DILs (daughters-in-law) to designate our children's spouses or significant others, but all traditions apply equally to SILs (sons-in-law). And FILs (fathers-in-law) as well as MILs (mothers-in-law). If that's confusing, turn off the TV, your cell phone, and your video game, then reread this paragraph at least four times. We're never too old to learn.

The Twelve Sacred Traditions of Magnificent Mothers-in-Law

Tradition One:

Magnificent MILs Cut the Apron Strings

**"Suddenly, you can't direct
their lives anymore."**

We love our children, yes we do—even if we don't like them. But once those children are married, Magnificent MILs realize that we must officially retire when it comes to directing their lives. This is as it should be, and not quite the sacrifice you might think. Retired people still have all their skills; they just don't have to go to work anymore. When specifically requested, though, they can still do consulting.

It's the same with rearing our kids. The minute the justice of the peace or the clergyman or the shaman says, "I now pronounce you," our motherly molding-and-shaping skills go *pouf!* and transform instantaneously into—gasp—meddling and nagging.

Magnificent MILs understand this and move on.

The newlyweds have each other now. Regardless of how poorly they might be managing, they have to make adjustments and learn their lessons for themselves. We cannot do it for them, and they will resent us if we try. Allow me to repeat that: they will resent us if we try.

It's imperative that we stop trying to tell them

what to do when they haven't asked for our advice. Though we have our children's best interests at heart, any unsolicited advice (the key word being *unsolicited*) qualifies as interference. We have to let go, scary as that is.

Even when a cherished son has married an emaciated pincushion of a DIL (daughter-in-law) who has a tongue stud and maroon hair, and was introduced by her roommate's cocaine dealer.

Or when a precious daughter (shudder) goes starry-eyed at the prospect of becoming bride number three for her father's alcoholic best friend.

Even if they lease a gas-guzzling SUV for five years, with only ten thousand miles a year allotted.

"Let them learn from their mistakes."

Even if they use the money they saved by getting food stamps to go on a Caribbean cruise.

Even when they "mark their bodies like the heathens" and/or get assorted metal objects inserted into their anatomies.

Even when they work all the time and live in a small apartment, but get a Great Dane puppy anyway, then don't have time to train it properly. (We are not, however, required to do it for them, or to dog sit.)

Even when they decide to go to the other in-laws' for Christmas. (Choke. Sob.)

The exception that proves the rule: The one time this rule doesn't apply is when there might be abuse involved. A Magnificent MIL never turns a blind eye to evidence that indicates abuse, even if it points to her own child.

If a MIL has good reason to suspect this serious problem in any form, she won't share her suspicions with anybody until she's consulted with a local shelter or agency to get solid information about the best course of action.

Tempting though it may be if the SIL is suspected of abuse, Magnificent MILs do *not* take the law into their own hands.

If any man *ever* beat my daughter, I'd want to grab my granddaddy's shotgun and do some rough justice, then and there. Wanting to do that is normal. Doing it isn't.

This is America, and people are innocent till convicted by a court of law, even if we catch them in the act.

That doesn't stop Magnificent MILs from creative problem solving. I know of a MIL who responded to her abused daughter's frantic call for help by calling 9-1-1, only to be told the police would be thirty minutes getting to her daughter's house. Frantic, she raced over there to find her child bruised and bleeding, and the drunk, abusive husband passed out on the kitchen floor, stark naked except for a dish towel placed over his privates by her daughter.

Lacking any rope to tie him with, this enterprising MIL drizzled most of a six-pack of instant glue onto the seat and back of a sturdy wooden kitchen chair. With her daughter's help, she hoisted the louse into the chair, covered his privates with the lightly glued dishtowel, then held him tightly against the chair till the glue set up. Just to make sure he couldn't do any further damage before the police got there, she pulled his hands behind the back of the chair and neatly glued his palms and fingers together as if in prayer, but aimed in a direction more appropriate to his bad behavior.

To spare the terrified children from seeing their father that way, she gagged him loosely with a pair of Sunset Tan pantyhose, then draped a clean king-sized sheet over him, thereby earning the Betty Crocker Seal of Approval.

She then tended to her daughter and helped pack up the children and belongings.

Personally, I call that just plain elegant, proof that the crassest of components can make up a deliciously delicate whole. From what I hear, the police, who didn't get there till an hour after her call, thought so, too.

The only trouble was, the chair wouldn't fit into the squad car, so they had to send for a paddy wagon.

The arraignment in Cobb County night court is now a legend.

"The 'no meddling' rule vanishes in this case."

❦ ❦ ❦ ❦

"Hitting is not acceptable in a marriage. Ever. Not even once. Not even when you do the hitting. Throw wet washrags, instead. Nobody gets hurt, but it gets your point across. If you're really mad, use ice water."

—*My Granny Bess*

Tradition Two

Magnificent MILs
Wake Up and Smell the Coffee
about their Married Children
and about Themselves.

"You cannot clean up their house for them."

Magnificent MILs have the courage to take a long, hard, objective look at our children's behaviors. All excuses are off. Never mind the cute little kids they used to be, or how many problems might have warped their tender little psyches.

Sure, blood is thicker than water. But Magnificent MILs are not afraid to ask ourselves, "What are the consequences of my child's choices?" and "Why am I still making excuses for my adult child's bad choices?"

The same annoying character flaws that made us grit our teeth as we brought up our kids have now become habits that affect their relationships. Despite our own shortcomings as parents, Magnificent MILs realize that grown children—however frail or needy—must take responsibility for their actions.

My precious (and politely passive-aggressive) MIL actually apologized to me for not making my only-child husband pick up his dirty clothes, confessing that she'd figured she could put up with it till he got married, but the woman who stole him away from her would have to pick up after him for the rest of his life. She said she'd never dreamed she'd love me so much.

You gotta love a woman who could be so up-front about her only child's flaws, much less her own sly motives for not correcting him.

Acknowledging our children's flaws doesn't mean we condone them, but it helps Magnificent MILs to understand what our DILs (daughters-in-law) must cope with.

WARNING: Seeing our children objectively doesn't mean we should point out those faults, especially to them. On the contrary. Our children already know their faults, and all too well. As do their spouses. (See Tradition Three.)

So when precious son Billy is always "too tired from work" to take out the garbage or put his clothes in the hamper, or rinse out the sink after he shaves or brushes his teeth, face it: He's a slob. He and his wife will have to work that out, without any input from you.

Or when our pampered princes refuse to eat anything except Pop Tarts, burgers, fries, hot dogs, pizza, and beer, they're not discriminating eaters, they're criminal eaters, and picky, picky, picky. Again—a topic to be worked out on their own.

Or when our married kids ignore the dirty dishes, overflowing trashcans, and soiled clothes piling up all over their house, they're not being laid back. They're flunking Household Hygiene 101. And we *definitely* don't need to get involved in that situation, either.

What we *do* need is to be honest with ourselves about our own behavior.

Magnificent MILs get honest about the things *we* do.

"Keep their faults to yourself."

When our kids get married, love means minding our own business, not theirs. The truth is, our maternal need to know what's going on with our children doesn't justify prying. If they want us to know something, trust me, they'll tell us.

We may mean well, but interference is interference, and our best intentions often hide a nasty little hidden agenda, even from ourselves.

Parental criticism isn't always direct. Many "innocent" questions are really criticisms. Example: "Have you found a pest control company to take care of the fleas in this place from that dog of yours?" Or: "Where do you want me to put the dirty dishes? The sink and the dishwasher are already full." Another zinger: "Don't you *smell* that?" Or: "How often do you take out the garbage?" Or: "When are you going to put that baby on some cereal, so she can sleep?" (Parenting decisions are a real mine-field.) Those aren't really questions. They're criticisms politely wrapped in so-called concern.

There's a huge difference between "Looks like you could sure use some help keeping this place decent," and "Taking care of a home is a big job. If you ever want your dad and me to come over and help, please don't hesitate to call. We'll set a date when we can all work together, then bring lunch and do things your way."

Another important point about questions: If we've asked a question clearly and not gotten an answer, trust me, they heard us the first time. Failure to respond is a good indication that we've stepped over the line, in which case, Magnificent MILs good-naturedly admit we slipped up, then we back off, pronto.

Actions speak louder than words, so when it comes to actions, Magnificent MILs are especially careful of the messages our behaviors send.

☙☙ ☙☙ ☙☙ ☙☙ ☙☙

"You can't love people in pieces. It's a package deal, and nobody's perfect."

—*My Granny Bess*

☙☙ ☙☙ ☙☙ ☙☙ ☙☙

Dogs mark their territory by whizzing on the bushes. Women do it by placing furniture and accessories, and setting their own housekeeping standards. So no Magnificent MIL would ever dream of declaring herself top dog in her married child's home by moving a chair or a lamp or an accessory without being asked. Nor would she "help out" by reorganizing anything without a specific invitation. Not only does that declare, "This is *my* territory, not yours," but it also shouts out loud and clear, "And you're not doing it right!"

Controlling our urges to interfere may require sedatives, hypnosis, and/or behavior modification therapy, but it's well worth the effort to keep from alienating our SILs or DILs. If those methods don't work, we can always try cold showers, briskly walking the dog, or having a margarita . . . or two, max. (Compulsive behavior and too much alcohol are a deadly mix.)

"Sometimes you just have to keep quiet."

Tradition Three:

Magnificent MILs are Consistently Kind.

**"Be nice. Make friends.
Go shopping together."**

Kindness always counts, even if your DIL spends five nights a week at the pool hall, or she dresses like a hooker. Or she really *was* a hooker before they married. The worse our DILs are, the kinder we need to be and the harder we need to reinforce whatever positives we can find. True kindness makes people feel special and worthy, and even small gestures can accomplish that. Magnificent MILs show our DILs that we value them as persons of worth and believe in their potential. That doesn't mean being a door mat. It means being considerate, even when our DILs aren't.

Kindness also extends to being compassionate about our DILs' faults. Magnificent MILs look beyond those faults for something to love. After one of my friend's fifty-something brothers married a twenty-three-year-old, size-two female bartender nicknamed "Pudge," his mother, a Magnificent MIL, said that if there was room in her son's heart for that woman, there would be room in hers. She did, however, unconsciously call her new DIL "Purge" for the brief duration of that disastrous marriage. We are, after all, only human.

Kindness means being thoughtful, going beyond what we're obligated to do. Thoughtfulness isn't a genetic trait. It takes work and planning. Magnificent MILs make the investment of time and effort to show in concrete ways that we care. We plan ways to practice kindness and work very hard at making our DILs feel special.

One way Magnificent MILs make that happen is by learning their DILs' sizes; favorite foods and restaurants; taste in TV, movies, music, and clothes; pet peeves; interests; favorite activities (even if it's watching wrestling); wish lists; accomplishments; and birthdays. Armed with that information, great MILs know what gifts to buy them and what foods to serve them when we entertain our in-laws (not to be confused with our out-laws, who are our DILs' parents).

Small things like sending occasional funny greeting cards can go a long way toward making people we care about feel loved and special. (Mushy or mean cards are a no-no. Keep it light and fun.)

❦❦ ❦❦ ❦❦ ❦❦

"A mother's a mother till she's six feet under. Till then, she'll keep trying to adjust your hair, your wardrobe, and your spending habits."

—*Haywood*

Tradition Four:

Magnificent MILs Set and Respect Reasonable Boundaries.

Setting clear, firm, reasonable bound-aries is a must for healthy relationships, but Magnificent MILs are kind when we state those boundaries. We mean what we say, but we're not mean when we say it. No matter how many times those boundaries are tested, we remain pleasant but firm. (We may have to scream into a pillow to blow off steam after the fact, but we don't fly off the handle.)

Kindness doesn't mean we put up with unacceptable behavior. Far from it. Magnificent MILs do not tolerate intolerable behavior. That's why we set reasonable boundaries. Wise MILs know better than to deny our children or their spouses the wisdom that comes from experiencing appropriate consequences for their actions. It's no kindness to rescue them from those consequences. That merely perpetuates the problem. So we're not required to bail them out for a DUI when they blew a 2.1 on the breathalyzer.

The quality of our communication has nothing to do with our intentions, and everything to do with the response our words provoke. So instead of "you" statements, Magnificent MILs use "I" statements, such as, "I'm not comfortable with clipping toenails in the living room during conversations. The bathroom is just down the hall." That's much more effective than, "Gross! Stop that! Were you brought up in a barn?" (Which we may be thinking, but we don't say.)

A great example of tactfully setting boundaries comes from a Magnificent MIL whose married daughter and son-in-law were home for Christmas. In the middle of the night, the groggy MIL headed for the only bathroom of her little house.

**"Handle tricky situations
with a good laugh."**

Halfway there, she was scared witless by the unexpected sight of her stark-naked son-in-law exiting the bathroom. She let out a shriek of alarm, then turned her back to him and laughed hysterically while he bolted for a towel and apologized. When she could manage to speak, she said over her shoulder, "I'm so sorry to inconvenience you, dear, but your father-in-law and I are pretty old-fashioned about things like nudity. In our house, we all wear clothes whenever we leave our rooms. I hope you'll understand."

He said "Yes, ma'am."

"Wonderful," she replied. "Why don't we just keep this between you and me? I wouldn't want to embarrass anybody, least of all you." And she never mentioned it again, even to her husband—who had slept through the whole thing. Now, *that's* a Magnificent MIL.

(She did eventually tell me, but only after the nudist SIL dumped her daughter for his secretary.)

Respecting boundaries:

"She's not peculiar, she just doesn't share your taste."

The flip side of setting boundaries means Magnificent MILs must also respect those set by their children and their spouses.

If her DIL is a vegan, the thoughtful MIL doesn't cook her famous pole beans with pork and then take it out and lie about it. She quietly prepares a small pot just for her DIL with vegetable bullion for flavor, and she doesn't embarrass her DIL by making a big deal out of it.

If her DIL is a Yankee who prefers Pepsi to Coca-Cola, a Magnificent MIL will purchase a generous supply (Here in Atlanta—the home of Coca-Cola—that may require a trip across town in the dead of night for discretion's sake.), then she'll make sure some are chilled and ready whenever her DIL comes to visit.

Or if a DIL is an animal rights person, a Magnificent MIL will temporarily replace the twelve-point buck's head in the den with a decorative wreath during visits, so as not to upset her son's wife. Even so, the thoughtful MIL is not obligated to donate her furs to the Salvation Army. She just doesn't wear them in her DIL's presence.

Such consideration goes a long way with both our children and our DILs. At best, they'll respond well to clear boundaries coupled with nonjudgmental love, even if it takes a while to bring them around. At worst, we MILs will end up looking good by comparison.

ভ্ভে ভ্ভে ভ্ভে ভ্ভে ভ্ভে

"I was lucky. I got my magnificent mother-in-law in the divorce."

—*Haywood*

Tradition Five:

Magnificent MILs are Loyal, Even When They have Good Reason Not to Be.

"Don't share your criticisms with your friends."

Poisoning other people's opinions about our children's spouses does nobody any good, and the fact is, we make ourselves look worse for criticizing them than they ever do for failing our expectations. Taking the high road is never a mistake, even when it requires gnashing of teeth, knuckle biting, or a swish of alum to keep our mouths shut. If our SILs or DILs are really horrible—and many are—everybody will end up reading about it in the paper, anyway, and we'll come out with a clear conscience and a grateful child.

Loyalty means believing there's hope for our DILs or SILs, no matter how many times they might let us down. It also means keeping private family information private. Magnificent MILs don't talk out of school about DIL's or SIL's shortcomings or problems, on penalty of losing all our teeth.

Just to be safe, we don't discuss any sensitive topics on our cell phones. You never know when the bored Buckaroo three cars back in the gridlock might be entertaining himself with an illegal cell scanner. My luck, it would be my SIL's best friend. I mean, look what happened to Princess Di when somebody picked up her oogy-woogy conversations with her lover. Not a good thing.

Further, loyalty demands that Magnificent MILs do not betray confidences or discuss our DILs' financial or health conditions, even among our closest friends, without permission. Such personal and private information is theirs to tell, not ours. If we're tempted to blab, we write everything down on a piece of paper, then burn it in the fireplace or sink. That exercise has saved me from myself many times.

Sometimes even innocent sharing can cause terrible hurt. A usually Magnificent MIL sat across the booth from me in a nice restaurant and confided how worried she was because her SIL's cocaine habit was draining her daughter's emotional and financial resources, and kept him from holding down a job. When we got up to leave, we discovered that his parents were in the next booth. Judging from the anguish on their faces, they'd had no idea what was going on.

๑๑ ๑๑ ๑๑ ๑๑ ๑๑

"Even when happiness is based on illusion, it still counts, long after the illusion is dead and buried."

—Haywood

Tradition Six:

Magnificent MILs
Bite Their Tongues:

"A word said is never dead."

It does nobody any good to point out the dents and high mileage on your married child's new previously owned car.

Nor does it help, after they've already closed on their new house (which they didn't tell us about because we're "always so nosy"), to inform the proud new homeowners that they got such a great deal because the lovely pasture backing up to their property is the site of the new county sewer plant. They'll find out, and when they do, Magnificent MILs never rub it in.

Magnificent MILs keep a lot of things to themselves—first and foremost, any mention of our children's past loves, engagements, or romances. We button our lips, especially when a child remarries, even if he or she lost a beloved spouse to death. Remember Mrs. Danvers in *Rebecca*. Not a pretty picture.

Sometimes, love means never having to say your daughter's last fiancé was handsomer, more religious, and made a hell of a lot more money.

What is, is. And it isn't our kids' old flames, no matter how superior we might have considered them. So for diplomacy's sake, we Magnificent MILs put away photos of old loves and dead-file those days from memory and conversation.

Another challenge: No matter how much our children might bash their spouses to us in anger, Magnificent MILs know better than to encourage such conversations, much less join in, even by implication. One of my favorite quotes is, "The smoothest and most convincing liar is memory." There are always two sides to any story.

༂ ༂ ༂ ༂ ༂

"You will be forgiven by the same measure you forgive."

—*The Lord's Prayer, paraphrased*

༂ ༂ ༂ ༂ ༂

If a MIL agrees with her frustrated son that his wife is lazy as a snake on a rock, that same son is just as likely to repeat the comment as a weapon against his wife, but attribute it to the mother who agreed! Husband and wife will make up and forgive each other, but the DIL won't forgive her MIL's disloyalty. It will linger and fester.

So when our children unload about their spouses, it's time to break out one of our Magnificent

MILs' secret weapons: The thoughtful expression, followed by a concerned, "And how did that make you feel?" After they've answered fully, we say, "I see. Go on."

I had to practice that one a lot to keep from offering advice, instead of giving my son a safe place to vent about his girlfriends (potential SILs), which was all he wanted, really. After years of simply reacting in such situations, it took work for me to learn to slow down, think, and consider the consequences before I spoke. Yet I'm so glad I did. Respecting others has not only earned their respect, but also helped me respect myself, in turn.

Magnificent MILs also avoid the following potentially destructive topics of conversation:

"Put away those childhood scrapbooks."

"Cute" but embarrassing stories about our children's pasts. Nosebleeds, wetting beds, closing drawers on their little peckers, and burning worms come to mind.

Tattling on our children's failures, like the time she lost the spelling bee, or he forgot his lines in the fifth grade pageant, or she threw up on the keys at her first piano recital, or he didn't get into the fraternity he wanted, or she made a tumbling error that cost her gymnastics team a championship.

Exposing past or current bad habits or embar-

"Let them keep their secrets."

rassing medical conditions, such as biting his toenails as a kid, sucking her thumb, bumping his head on the crib till he went to sleep, her recent problems with flatulence, or the fact that milk still gives him diarrhea.

Discussing whatever dreams our children sacrificed to marry. This is just plain cruel.

Holding forth with detailed medical stories about anyone, especially tales that involve anything graphic or humiliating, like Aunt Minnie's hysterectomy or Grandpa's "prostrate" problems that explain the constant stain on his pants, or the vestigial twin the surgeon discovered inside your daughter when he took out her appendix. Yuk!

Discussing money matters, ours or theirs. Anything from complaining about not having enough money, to emphasizing how much we do have, to worrying out loud about the way they choose to spend theirs. Major no-no.

Revealing skeletons in the closet. Outing the criminals or nut cases hanging from our family trees won't help us get those grandchildren we crave. Such stories are more likely to prompt a tubal ligation.

Running down ex-spouses, ours or our children's, no matter how much they deserve it. If a MIL criticizes former sons- or daughters-in-law, her new ones will never trust her not to do the same thing to them.

❦❧ ❦❧ ❦❧ ❦❧ ❦❧

"Tickling is just a socially acceptable form of minor torture. And telling funny stories at somebody else's expense isn't funny; it's just plain mean."

—*My Granny Bess*

❦❧ ❦❧ ❦❧ ❦❧ ❦❧

So much for the things Magnificent MILs know but shouldn't talk about. Now we move on to the things we observe, but do not mention, or those we're tempted to damn with faint praise.

A strained acknowledgement of your new DIL's navel ring doesn't fool anyone. Criticism is criticism, even when it's couched in a frail compliment. When confronted by things we can't say anything nice about, Magnificent MILs employ another of our secret weapons: The raised eyebrows, Mona Lisa smile, and ambiguous "Hmmm."

Tip: It helps to practice the proper expression in the mirror to make sure that in extreme cases, our eyes don't cross and our emotions don't escape. Once we master this technique, it becomes one of our most effective tools.

As for all those pent-up frustrations we must conceal, Magnificent MILs save them for our regular MIL-Anon meetings (not to be confused with Mom-

Anon), where it's safe to vent as long as we keep the focus on ourselves and don't betray our children's trust.

My recovering alcoholic friend Pru gave me an Al-Anon bookmark titled, "Just for Today." All the simple, daily objectives were really good, but my favorite is the one that says, "Just for today, I will not criticize. No, not one bit."

Convicted, I took the challenge to heart, but boy, was it hard. I'd never thought of myself as a negative or judgmental person, but I soon discovered that I was. It took time and practice for me to break the habit, but when I did, I discovered that the world looked a lot brighter, and people were a lot friendlier.

ᎧᎧ ᎧᎧ ᎧᎧ ᎧᎧ ᎧᎧ

"A man who won't protect his wife from his mother isn't a man."

—*My Granny Bess*

Tradition Seven:

Magnificent MILs Give Only What and When They Can Truly Give.

This involves several things.
First, parents should only give our children what we can reasonably afford to give. Ending up destitute, even if we were trying to help, does them no favors. Nor does mortgaging our houses for bail.

Second, we should make certain that our gift is welcome. Never mind that Grandma's fabulous four-layer yellow cake with fudge frosting took all day to make from scratch and is your son's favorite. It's not a gift to take him one if your DIL is on a diet. It's sabotage. And torture. Inviting your son over alone for some is fine, but undermining anybody's effort to lose weight is passive-aggressive dirty pool.

Third, it isn't generous to give our DILs presents, regardless of the cost, that imply their tastes leave something to be desired. Gifts like that aren't gifts. They're sly efforts to impose the giver's tastes and preferences.

Treating our midriff-baring DILs to conservative clothes won't make them see the light. Nor will surprising the newlyweds with a leather Lazy Boy sofa to replace their low, uncomfortable contemporary one that's so hard to get onto and up from.

Fourth: Homemade crafts fall into their own perilous category. Just because our DILs compliment the weeping clowns we did in oil painting class, that doesn't mean they want to hang them in their living rooms. Or even their attics. This isn't pre-communist China. When somebody admires something, we're not obligated to give it to them. They may have just been being polite or trying to make us feel good.

Magnificent MILs don't press their creations on anybody, because the recipients might be afraid to refuse for fear of hurting our feelings. It's a lot more considerate to make it clear to our married children they only have to ask for a homemade creation, and we'll hand it over or do one to order.

Fifth: Magnificent MILs never give anything, personal or for the house, that strongly reflects individual taste unless it's an exact item our children or their spouses have said they'd like to have. So if your kids' place looks like a page out of the Pottery Barn catalogue, ix-nay on the ainting-pay of the poker-playing dogs.

Looking for inspiration? A few weeks before my birthday or the holidays, my own Magnificent MIL would offer to treat me to lunch if I'd accompany her as she shopped. While we were taking care of whatever she needed, she paid close attention to the things I admired for myself—from an inexpensive pair of earrings to a beautiful suit she insisted I try on. Then she discreetly had the clerk hold whatever items she wanted to give me till she could come back and buy them. So my birthday and Christmas presents were always a surprise, and a welcome one.

With the exception of treasured heirlooms our children have specifically requested (which we may make clear are theirs to preserve for posterity), a true gift never has strings attached. No conditions. Nada.

When Magnificent MILs give gifts, we make sure the recipients understand that those gifts are theirs to do with as they please, even if that means exchanging, returning, or giving them away. Since most gift receipts do not entitle the recipient to a refund, thoughtful MILs make a copy of the receipt for their own records, then include the original with the gift, tucked into a sealed envelope marked, "Open only in the event of return."

The exception that proves the rule: The one exception to giving without strings attached is loaning money, in which case the conditions must be mutually agreeable (without any pressure or manipulation) and spelled out in writing in plain English, including terms of payment and specific consequences for late payments or default. All parties should get a fully signed and dated set of papers.

No papers = no loan. And that means no, "Sure, we'll sign them later, but we need the cash today." Your friendly local lawyer or reputable computer legal software can provide the necessary wording or forms. Magnificent MILs know that good documents help preserve good relationships. More families than you can shake a stick at have been split apart by differing interpretations when money changes hands.

&: &: &: &: &:

"If you want to be happy, no grudges allowed!"

—*My Granny Bess*

Tradition Eight:

Magnificent MILs Never Wear Out Their Welcome.

"Always call ahead."

Healthy contact with our married kids is easy to maintain if we stick to a few crucial guidelines.

Mainly, we should ask our DILs and SILs to be frank about when and how often they feel comfortable with our calling them or getting together. If we abide by their wishes, we might be able to throw in an impromptu invitation occasionally, as long as we're willing to take no for an answer.

Visits:

Magnificent MILs always make visits special, whether we treat our married children and their spouses to a favorite homemade meal, or dinner at their favorite restaurant, or a movie they've been wanting to see.

Magnificent MILs *always* call ahead (at least an hour) before visiting. "I'm parked in your driveway," doesn't count. And when we call, we make it easy for our DILs to take a rain check. Better: "I'm going to be near your place in about an hour, and I'd love to drop by and see you and baby for a few minutes"— translate: for half an hour, max, unless invited to stay longer—"if that's convenient for you. If not, when would be a good time this week?" This works only if we cheerfully accept their verdicts and abide by the time limits.

Just to make sure she's welcomed with open arms, one Magnificent MIL always brings a home-made treat that fits with her DIL's post-baby diet, even if it's just a small salad. Another stops by the flower stand for a few of her DIL's favorite sunflowers on the way. But even if you come bearing gifts, you still have to call ahead.

What if our children or their spouses don't check their messages or remember to turn their phones on? First, that's a clear signal that MIL may have already worn out her welcome. But it's never too late to sit down in person and hash out some ground rules, making it clear that those rules are to make sure we don't impose.

Magnificent MILs say, "I really want to make sure that my visits are convenient for you," then ask for suggestions about how that can be worked out. If our kids only want to see us once a month, we grin and bear it, and make sure those visits are special and enjoyable for them. (See Tradition Nine.)

When we come from out of town to visit, and our children's guest accommodations are limited, Magnificent MILs cheerfully book a nearby hotel or motel, or find other friends or family to stay with. The operative word is cheerful, which rules out heavy sighs or complaints about the bad beds or highway noise at the hotel. No martyring in general! (See Tradition Ten.)

🐞 🐞 🐞 🐞 🐞

"What do you mean, call before I come over? I'm still your mother. I should suddenly become premeditated, just because you left home?"

—*Wedding Belles*

🐞 🐞 🐞 🐞 🐞

As far as how much and what kind of contact our children prefer, my friend Teeny's local DIL likes to be taken out once a month for lunch to a nice restaurant. My friend Linda has her daughter Abby and Osama Damned Son-in-law (a term she only uses with her best friends) over every other Sunday afternoon for homemade comfort food they can all enjoy—not just Abby's favorites, but a few of Osama's favorite dishes that fit in with his Moslem/Rasta dietary beliefs. Linda even put a personal ad in a local Arab-American newspaper asking for English translations of his favorite Iranian dishes, so now she can fix several things just like Mama-sama made.

Calling the out-laws (his or her parents) and asking how to make their child's favorite foods earns

Magnificent MILs huge brownie points all around—unless, as in the case of Osama, the outlaws have declared their child officially dead for marrying yours.

Telephone calls:

When it comes to calling our kids and their spouses, the content of our phone calls, not just the frequency, is key to whether or not they screen us out with Caller ID or relegate us to the message center they consistently ignore. Several brief, upbeat calls a week at times convenient to our children are guaranteed to be more welcome than less frequent marathons.

"Less is more, in terms of phone calls."

YAK YAK
YAK YAK YAK

Want to know if you're calling too much? A great first step can be an eye-opener: check a print-out of your phone records for a month or two. Cell phone bills usually include a detailed call record. Land-line call lists might cost a little, but it's worth the investment.

After my son and DIL moved back to our neighborhood, I thought I was being really good about not bothering them unnecessarily . . . till I got my cell phone bill. Page after page, I saw where I'd dialed their number, totaling seventy—count 'em, seventy—entries in all! Granted, a lot of them were times they didn't answer, so I hung up before the message came on, but their records will show all those calls, too. Ouch.

So now, whenever I'm tempted to phone over something trivial, I simply remind myself about the sinking chill I felt when I saw all those entries staring at me in black and white, and I curb the urge.

When it *is* okay to call, Magnificent MILs always identify ourselves by name, right off the bat, as in, "Hi, Wade. It's Georgia." Not, "Hi. It's me." Which is not only rude, but also bad grammar.

If our DILs answer the phone when we're calling for our sons or grandchildren, we pay attention to her before asking her to pass the phone along.

Next? "Is this a good time for you to talk?" If they say no, we ask when to call back, then abide by what they say. If they say yes, we keep it cheerful and to the point. Magnificent MILs save leisurely chats for "my treat" lunches or dinners at their favorite spots.

Magnificent MILs don't repeat themselves in phone conversations. Once said is enough. More is nagging, as discussed earlier.

When it comes to old business, we let them bring it up. No Magnificent MIL would ever ask, "Did you call the bank to check on that equity line I told you about last week? Those low interest rates won't last forever." Frankly, no Magnificent MIL would have mentioned the equity line in the first place.

Family conflicts: When speaking with our children or their spouses, Magnificent MILs keep them well out of family difficulties that don't involve them. Gossiping, family or not, is off limits. When Magnificent MILs are in conflict with anyone, they deal directly and privately with the individual involved. They don't put children or their spouses in the middle. Nor do they insert themselves into conflicts that married children might have with siblings or other family members. If children or their spouses try to draw a Magnificent MIL into things, she listens, then smiles and says, "I'm so sorry you two are having a bad time. I love you both, and I know you'll be able to work it out."

Speaking of phone calls, Magnificent MILs don't waste anyone's time with things they can do on their own. Asking for a referral to a plumber is fine; keeping our DIL on the line while we conference call for an appointment is not. (One MIL I know actually did this, then was amazed when her DIL grew impatient.)

It's easier to grill people over the phone than face-to-face, but it's never good behavior. So Magnificent MILs never use phone calls to ask embarrassing questions. (See Tradition Two.) Example: "Are you still taking the pill? I thought you said you were going to give me a grandbaby." Now on to another challenge.

❧❧ ❧❧ ❧❧ ❧❧ ❧❧

"When it comes to marriage, don't set your sights *too* high, honey. The best man in the world is still just a man."

—*Wedding Belles*

Tradition Nine:

Magnificent MILs Respect Their DILs' and SILs' Allergies, Preferences, Special Diets and Limitations.

KILLING KITTENS
ROCK BAND

**"Perhaps your SIL is simply
allergic to soap."**

Magnificent

MILs realize that making our SILs or DILs miserable will make our children miserable, too. We'll turn ourselves inside-out to keep our children's loyalties from being torn between us and their mate. So we are careful to accommodate their spouses' needs and limitations. General Allergies:

Allergies, even minor ones, are no laughing matter, especially when it comes to our DILs.

After I admired the beautiful, prize-winning lilies John's mama grew in her garden, she made a special arrangement for the table the first time she had me over for dinner. The trouble is, while I think lilies are beautiful, I'm really allergic to them in close quarters. Afraid I might hurt her feelings by asking her to take the arrangement away, I soldiered on through the wonderful meal she'd prepared, unable to taste a thing because of my runny eyes, runny nose, and hovering asthma that signaled its presence with a dry cough that made me feel like my lungs had poison ivy.

John asked me if I was okay, and when I politely

said I was, he took me at my word and went back to the conversation he was having with his father (such a man-erism).

Within five minutes, though, I became so ill that my precious MIL finally realized what was happening. "Oh my goodness!" she said. "You poor dear. It's the lilies, isn't it?" When I nodded, she hastily whisked the flowers, vase and all, into a large covered trashcan in the kitchen, apologizing profusely.

It could have been excruciating for both of us, but she, God bless her, marched cheerfully back into the dining room and started scooping up the bowls of food. "Come on," she said, "It's a beautiful evening outside. Let's have a picnic on the screened porch. It'll be fun." And it was.

So every time I think of the lily fiasco, instead of feeling humiliated, I just love John's mama more.

Food Allergies:

When it comes to food allergies, Magnificent MILs never assume that "just a little bit" won't hurt an allergic DIL.

I once watched a woman in a now-defunct Buckhead restaurant swell up and turn the color of a Weimaraner after diving into what was supposed to be a shrimp-free salad, when in fact, the cooks had just picked the baby shrimp garnish out of one they'd already made. Fortunately, the ambulance arrived in minutes, but the paramedics were doing a hasty tracheotomy as they carted her out.

So no cheating. Our DILs might not have such an extreme reaction, but even small amounts of forbidden foods can have a cumulative effect on most allergies. Magnificent MILs check product labels and bend over backward to make sure the meals they serve their DILs are safe, and the choices fit with their tastes and dietary requirements. Even if we think the diet they're on is silly.

If the allergy is a minor one and our child's spouse decides to risk a sinus headache by eating a banana split, a Magnificent MIL holds her peace and doesn't keep score.

Pet Allergies:

Now, to the volatile topic of pets. Muffy the sheepdog may have been a member of your family a lot longer than your in-law, but if your child's spouse has pet allergies, even vigorous vacuuming probably won't make your home safe for a visit.

At the very least, pets should be confined well away from the person who's allergic. That means *away*, not in a nearby room where everyone can hear Muffy scratching and barking and whining to get out, which makes everybody miserable.

Magnificent MILs realize that it doesn't fool anybody to leave Muffy out and holler, "Muffy! Here!" or "Leave that nice girl alone." That sends a huge passive-aggressive message that the dog matters more than the guest. (Which may be true, but Magnificent MILs never show it.)

If a MIL can't bear to send her pets to a neighbor's or lock them securely in the garage or the back yard, she has the option of taking the kids out to a restaurant they like, or offering to bring dinner to their house. (Just make sure there's no pet hair on or in the food. Can we say, "Acckkk!?)

Magnificent MILs (and magnificent hostesses of any kind) never put their pets' comfort over their guests'. And Magnificent MILs *never,* and I mean *never* take their pets along when visiting unless both host and hostess specifically request it, without prompting or wheedling. Nor do Magnificent MILs put on their martyr's crowns when they have to make arrangements to clear the house or board Muffy so allergic guests will be comfortable and feel welcome.

If that's hard, just ask yourself, "Do I love my child more than I love the dog?"

Well, maybe that's not the best question to ask yourself, since the answer might well be, "No." A better question might be, "Do I want my child to think I love him/her more than I love the dog?"

🐞🐞 🐞🐞 🐞🐞 🐞🐞 🐞🐞

"Allowing somebody to take advantage of you doesn't help anybody; it just makes you their partner in crime."

—*My Granny Bess*

🐞🐞 🐞🐞 🐞🐞 🐞🐞 🐞🐞

Smoking and Drinking:

When it comes to alcohol (and other "relaxers"), Magnificent MILs and FILs (fathers-in-law) are always considerate when visiting. If our children don't keep liquor in the house, we should not insult them by bringing our own unless they specifically invite us to. (No hinting allowed!)

When hosting, Magnificent MILs always provide favorite non-alcoholic beverages for non-drinkers and wouldn't dream of embarrassing them by making a big to-do about giving them soft drinks when everyone else has "real" drinks or wine.

If SILs or DILs are recovering alcoholics, it's *not* okay for us to bring that up. Past or present problems with alcohol or drugs are theirs, not ours, to tell. And even if they do open the subject, Magnificent MILs still refrain from doing so themselves.

Nor is it okay for us to entertain the table with tales of drunken Uncle Willy's escapades or fond reminiscences of our own.

Speaking of getting high: Magnificent MILs don't get drunk when entertaining or visiting their married children. Ever.

Nor do they refill their guests' drinks or wine without asking first, and they cheerfully take no for an answer.

Magnificent MILs always provide food with cocktails, and they pace refills to discourage guests from overindulging, which invariably results in disaster.

If married children ask Magnificent MILs not to drink or smoke in their homes, good MILs and FILs cheerfully agree. No martyring or complaining allowed. (See Tradition Ten.)

If parents can't manage a few smokeless hours for the sake of good family relations (though most smokers seem to manage fine for airline flights), they should resort to a nicotine patch or ask *both* their hosts if it's okay to smoke somewhere outside. If the answer's yes, they choose a spot that's well away from doors and windows, and make sure to put ashes and butts into a fireproof container that can be doused with water, then discarded into a sealed garbage container so the odor won't inconvenience anybody.

One of the biggest sources of conflict is MILs or FILs smoking or drinking around their grandchildren when the parents have asked them not to. It's not a question of grandparents' rights in their own homes, but their grandchildren's health. Magnificent MILs and FILs love their grandchildren enough to give them clean air to breathe and clear-headed attention when we're with them.

Conversely, we MILs have the same right to ask our married children and their spouses not to smoke in our homes. But we should be considerate and set up a place for them to smoke outside, then schedule things to allow them to do so without missing out on important holiday activities.

෯෯ ෯෯ ෯෯ ෯෯ ෯෯

"It's a good thing God doesn't let us know what's going to happen. If He did, we might never get out of bed."

—*Wedding Belles*

Tradition Ten:

Magnificent MILs don't martyr.

"Never be a martyr."

There are no exceptions. If we agree to do anything that makes us resentful, the problem is ours and ours alone.

When we let anybody, including our children, to take advantage of us, they're not causing our unhappiness. We are, by not knowing how to say "no" when our instincts warn us we should. It's not selfish to say a firm but kind "I'm sorry, but that's a lot more than I can handle," when asked to keep all four toddlers so both our daughters and their spouses can spend two weeks at Club Med. In that case, saying "no" is a matter of survival—both the Magnificent MIL's and the grandchildren's.

My best friends and I made an actual martyr's crown out of a jeweled, gold-toned adjustable plastic coronet I got at the costume shop. We decorated it with big, fake tear-drop diamonds and artificial flowers with fake dew (tears) on the petals. We finished it off with several soulful, pocket-sized portraits of martyred saints, and cartoon-caption phrases that said, "Woe is me," and "Nobody appreciates me." Whenever one of us starts acting put-upon, out comes the crown for a mandatory coronation at the nearest mirror. I challenge anybody to wallow in self-pity confronted with that. Since I have custody of the thing, I even use it at home to cheer myself up when I start feeling exploited.

But since everybody's not crafty, and we don't always have our crown around, we Magnificent MILs have devised an official response whenever any of us feels compelled to wallow in self-pity: "Do you need twenty-four hours to whine about this, or forty-eight?" Whereby the martyr in question must pick one, then abide by the time frame.

The truth is, most MIL martyrs aren't nailed to their crosses. They climb right up there, uninvited, then fret and wail about the results. Like my friend Molly the Martyr (names have been changed to protect the guilty), a professional faux-painter who insisted on doing her son's entire new house "as a housewarming gift," despite her DIL's worried objections, only to get furious when her DIL asked her to redo the fake-stone powder room in something more cheery than dark, gray-green castle stones and ivy. (See Tradition Seven, paragraph two.)

But sometimes, even Magnificent MILs have lapses. Not too often, or we blow our credibility entirely, but hey, everybody makes mistakes. When we do slip, we don't beat ourselves up about it. (Masochism and martyrdom combine to become a passive-aggressive's favorite stealth weapon.) We admit we were wrong, then make a sincere effort to do better.

Seeing and admitting we're wrong goes a long way with DILs and SILs.

If a Magnificent MIL can't do something with a free and open heart, she shouldn't do it at all, even though that makes her uncomfortable. Those "bad girl" guilt vibes we feel when we act on our gut instincts that say "no" are understandable, since most of us have spent our married lives taking care of everybody within a mile, whether or not they wanted us to. But feelings aren't facts.

So when a son begs his mother to teach his new wife (who works just as demanding a schedule as he does) how to make all his favorite dishes just like Mama did, Mama shouldn't say "yes," just because he asked. That could cause a lot of resentment on her side and her DIL's. But if Mama's a Magnificent MIL who's willing to pass on her tips and tricks, she can earn her DIL's undying gratitude by saying, "If this is her idea, I'd be delighted. But if it's yours, I've got a better one: Why don't I teach *you* how to make them? That way, you can have them whenever you want. Come over Sunday afternoon, and we'll get started. You can take home whatever we cook." Then suggest his very favorite dish as a starter.

If that doesn't work, the MIL can just say no.

"Remember, it isn't just about YOUR feelings."

ᏬᏋ ᏬᏋ ᏬᏋ ᏬᏋ ᏬᏋ

"There are only two cures for heartache: Get over it, already, or die."

—*Wedding Belles*

Tradition Eleven:

Magnificent MILs Don't Expect People to Read Their Minds.

Speak up. No sulking permitted."

Oooh. That's a toughie. It isn't easy letting go of our childish fantasies that those who love us will automatically know what we want or what we're thinking. But Magnificent MILs grieve the loss of those unrealistic expectations and move on.

How many times have we all thought something like, "She knows I don't like seafood. Why did she suggest the Red Lobster?" or, "Hasn't that boy been paying the slightest bit of attention? I never wear perfume. Why did he give me perfume for Christmas?" or "How can they go to his family for Christmas two years in a row? Anybody knows you should take turns with Christmas!" (Never mind that you live a mile away and get to see your daughter anytime you want, but his huge family only gets him once a year.)

Magnificent MILs ask for what they want and speak up about their feelings in as positive a way as possible. Sulking is out. (See Tradition Ten, paragraph five.) Magnificent MILs act like real grown-ups, and grown-ups avoid disappointments by being up front about their expectations and taking responsibility for their own happiness.

Sometimes that means changing our expectations. When her children kept forgetting her birthday, one Magnificent MIL I know decided to celebrate by meeting them all, Dutch treat, at a moderately priced restaurant and springing for preordered birthday cake and ice cream. Then she distributed fun but inexpensive gifts she'd picked up at garage sales or dollar stores, then wrapped in Sunday comic sections. Bottom line, she gets to celebrate with her family, and everybody has a good time. Sure, she'd love to have them surprise her with a big party every year, but that expectation is as unrealistic as going to bed in Boston and hoping to wake up in Camelot next to Sean Connery. Ain't gonna happen.

Another Magnificent MIL sends postcards two weeks ahead of her birthday to her married children with "Buy Mom a funny birthday card," on the front. A week ahead, they receive one that says, "Mail mom's funny birthday card!"

If she doesn't get them, she sends the slackers funny cards, herself. And she sets a good example by sending their birthday and holiday cards on time.

The second part of the tradition involves being honest about what we're thinking. Nobody benefits when we harbor hurt feelings or stuff resentments, but we need to be careful how we share those feelings. Accusations help no one, but lightening up makes things easier for everybody. Magnificent MILs are honest about their feelings, but with a light touch. And they stick to the matter at hand. They don't keep a record of wrongs or drag up past difficulties.

One Magnificent MIL was deeply offended by her SIL's profanity, but instead of marshalling the wrath of God, she got creative. "Jason, honey, I know I'm old-fashioned," she said to him, "but it flies all over me when you take the Lord's name in vain that way. Do you think maybe you could say "Jujubes" or "Granola bars!" instead, when I'm around? I'd appreciate it so much." The next time he slipped, she grinned in mock surprise and said, "Jujubes? Did you just say jujubes?" It took a while, but he eventually got the message. And every time he said "Jujubes!" she laughed and thanked him.

۞ ۞ ۞ ۞ ۞

"Curiosity about somebody else's business is nothing but a bad mix of jealousy and not enough to do. It'll get you into trouble every time."

—Wedding Belles

Tradition Twelve:

Magnificent MILs are Flexible about Holiday Plans.

"Holidays are all about compromise."

Magnificent

MILs are creative about sharing our married children, and we know when to lighten up. Going to war about who gets the kids for Easter or Passover makes everybody miserable. The Solomon solution doesn't work, either.

What is a holiday, anyway? It's a symbolic observance on a special day. As long as the observance and the day are special, Magnificent MILs understand that observances don't have to take place on THE day everybody else celebrates. Or in the same way. Remember how hard it was for us to spread ourselves between family and in-laws when we were first married?

ලුණ ලුණ ලුණ ලුණ ලුණ

"Never underestimate an old woman. She's still a woman."

—*Wedding Belles*

Nobody can be two places at once, but two key concepts can make for happy holidays all around.

1. *Have a game plan that doesn't require clones for everybody to be happy.*

Just because things have always been a certain way, doesn't mean they have to stay that way. Magnificent MILs realize that our married children (particularly when they have children of their own) have a right to work out their own traditions, and we adjust our plans to accommodate theirs.

My Magnificent MIL came up with the brilliant idea of having everybody from his side of the family for Thanksgiving dinner on Wednesday night, instead of on Thursday. That way, we didn't have to worry about alternating holidays, giving up our own celebration, or offending my family.

My friend Sarah's mother decided to think out of the box, too. Weary from doing the traditional cutwork-table-cloth and good-china epic, her mom laid claim on the Sunday afternoon following Turkey Day for a paper-plate-and-plastic-utensils potluck of sandwich fixings and tailgate fare at her house. All six brothers and sisters and their families gathered for a great, but unconventional observance. The sports fans watched football, the rest visited and tended the buffet, and the kids bonded down in the rumpus room playing with each other's toys or trying to get high score on four old-fashioned arcade games their grandfather had from the VFW and had refurbished.

It doesn't have to be arcade games; anything out of the ordinary, no matter how hokey, can become a beloved tradition for the children: spirited tournaments of Hearts or Monopoly; table-wrecking games of Spoon; classic kids' movies we've all loved, enhanced with popcorn and theater-style candies. Even something as simple as letting the kids pick from a selection their parents' old favorite books for a story time with Grandpa can make the day memorable.

With Thanksgiving proper available, Sarah was free to follow her own tradition by helping feed the homeless in downtown Atlanta with the Hosea Williams dinner. So thanks to her mother, a Magnificent MIL, she and her family were able to celebrate an extended holiday that left them full in spirit as well as body.

Another option extended families have is choosing one particular B-list holiday to celebrate together. My friend Linda's mama arranges for her whole family to rent condos at Sanibel Island in Florida the week of July Fourth every summer, so all the cousins and aunts and uncles can stay close. Part of the fun is their annual clothes-swap, where kids' and grown-ups' like-new clothes and accessories change hands. Linda cleans out her closets and comes home with a fresh tan and new wardrobe every year. (Fastidious to the core, only-child husband Brooks declines to participate, and requires sedatives when the shoe-swap convenes, but daughter Abby claims it's her favorite holiday celebration of the year.)

It doesn't have to be condos. It could be camping, or meeting at a hired hall or favorite restaurant for a day of fun and catching up. The secret is making it fun and consistent.

2. Magnificent MILs make their holiday wishes known at least six months ahead (preferably the year before), and are willing to compromise.

That means asking what our married children want for their holidays, paying attention to their answers, and working out something we can all live with—well in advance, without undue pressure. We can be persistent, but guilt and manipulation are not allowed.

So no, "This will probably be your grandmother's last Christmas! I can't believe you'd just take off on a cruise like that." Never mind that Grandma hasn't recognized anybody for three years and takes off all her clothes the minute you turn your back.

Or, "Bridget's parents have three other children. You're our only one. What kind of a Christmas will it be for us without you? Nothing! We might as well forget the whole thing!" Even a Magnificent MIL might think this, but she doesn't use it as emotional blackmail.

Emotional blackmail never works, anyway. It just puts distance and resentment between us and the victims. Trust me, I know.

The little girl in all of us wants those we love to know what we need and provide it, but Magnificent MILs are grownups. Grownups ask for what they want, and their requests are considerate. And reasonable. Holidays are special if we make them that way, and a big part of that is making sure we're on the same page with our married children.

ᘘᘞ ᘘᘞ ᘘᘞ ᘘᘞ ᘘᘞ

"Being bitter is like drinking strychnine and expecting it to kill the other person."

—*My Granny Bess*

**"Be the mother-in-law
you wish you'd had."**

In Summary

We, best friends and founders of Mothers-in-Law Anonymous, have made the conscious choice to become the mothers-in-law we wish we'd had. The fact is, there are DILs and SILs from hell in this world. And there are competitive, irrational out-laws who can really throw a monkey wrench in the works. Those challenges qualify us for plenty of heartfelt "poor baby's," but they don't let us off the hook.

Fortunately, life is progress, not perfection, and we don't beat ourselves up when we fail. (See the Twelve Sacred Traditions of Friendship in *The Red Hat Club*). So we forge ahead.

Magnificent MILs know how to lighten up. They're flexible. They're realists, yet they remain positive. They set and respect boundaries—especially those involving door keys. They don't rescue their married children from the consequences of their mistakes, but neither do they bring those mistakes up. Last but not least, they operate from love, even when they don't get it back.

So much for the ideal. As for the rest of us, there's always Do Over—with apology, of course. (See the Twelve Sacred Traditions of Friendship in my novel, *The Red Hat Club.*) And the comfort of our fellow less-than-perfect MILs when we fall short.

The secret is to keep trying and to keep laughing.

ACKNOWLEDGMENTS

Thanks so much to BelleBooks for making this possible, especially to Sandra Chastain for her wisdom, help, and encouragement all these many years, and to my wonderful editor, Deborah Smith (no relation), whose luminous fiction has always been my inspiration. And thanks to Debra Dixon for letting me have pink.

Special thanks, also, to Jennifer Enderlin, my editor and associate publisher at St. Martin's Press, for her unfailing support and permission to use excerpts from my novels.

Made in the USA
Middletown, DE
08 December 2015